SAFETY NETS

SAFETY NETS

Poems

RED SQUIRREL PRESS

First published in 2021 by Red Squirrel Press
36 Elphinstone Crescent
Biggar
South Lanarkshire
ML12 6GU
www.redsquirrelpress.com

Layout, design and typesetting by Gerry Cambridge
e:gerry.cambridge@btinternet.com

A CIP catalogue record for this book is available from the
British Library.

ISBN: 978 1 913632 25 0

Red Squirrel Press is committed to a sustainable future.
This publication is printed in the UK by Imprint Digital
using Forest Stewardship Council certified paper.
www.digital.imprint.co.uk

Contents

For Tess Spencer

Pinch Stile

There are mornings when the door sticks
at the jamb, then opens a crack
on a day already threatened
by the radio litany—
violence, hurt and hatred.
When the first things you see
instead of wallflowers are
the soft clumps of down where
the sparrowhawk fed, bringing
death into your garden.

On these mornings your mind sticks—
more time has gone than is to come.
You know it, but dare not feel it.
The past spreads its patchwork landscape,
today your path is narrowing,
single track through a pinch stile.
Stop there. Inside you a girl still lives—
the one who flung doors open
as if each morning was a promise.
Let her go first. She knows the way.

Adopted

In spite of cornfields and stickleback ponds,
shingle beaches and salty winds,
she fell out of love with her birthplace.
It shrank between roads and factories,
having nothing more to say.

Now she rattles through this landscape
on a country bus and feels
a familiar tingling in her chest,
as if joy is bubbling up,
a lurch like love in her stomach.

The August fields spread out below—
every shade of yellow, bleached brown,
burnt orange. Roads meander,
villages hug the valleys,
and the land keeps stretching,
its colours singing.

What the Landscape Holds

A Tuesday passenger, I am accepted now
among the regulars—Valerie and Matt
at the Cornsay stop, and Vera, loud
in going-out clothes and lavish make-up,
at Old Esh—the *Scarlet Band* their daily escape
from heating bills and too much retirement,
rattling them off to Bishop and the Arnison.
I love the view—the landscape's folds and humps,
fields greening now, buds bursting.
Lambs skitter in gangs, hills soften
in the late spring warmth as if they had
always been pasture.
                      But does the past
hang on, I wonder, for my companions,
their childhood outlook ghosting the view—
the hills, rough slag heaps; instead of fields,
pits and coke ovens, chimneys spewing
into gritty air; the high cycle path
along the ridge, a viaduct with coal trucks
shaking the wooden struts, and engines
sending smoke to settle in a shroud
along the valley.
                      Beneath the surface—
where no one sees—among the roots,
machinery still rusts and crumbles,
and deeper still, water goes on finding
its way through long deserted tunnels.

On the site of Winterton Hospital, County Lunatic Asylum

The executive estate is finished,
detached dwellings solid in sunny stone.
The house buyers have all moved in.

They do not know yet how a wave
of sadness follows them along the hall,
how in the lounge they will start to hear

whispers, a cry, an angry shout,
how hunched figures are stilled in broken chairs
inside the new conservatory.

They will not understand the way
despair envelops them as they climb the stairs.
If they look out—where the bus stop used to be—

they may just see her standing,
an old woman in a washed-out nightdress.
She is waiting for the bus to take her home.

The Clogmaker's Son

Perhaps it was the new century
that let him go—or the way the railway
brought the city closer. He never wore
the sturdy clogs his father made.
He would not follow in those shoes.
The father's feet had only trod
the narrow alleyways of home.
His son began the wandering
from the family's settled place.

Science and mathematics moved
him on from north to south—he left
us nowhere to belong. Uprooted,
our hold is tenuous—we live
on land that doesn't know us.
To the question *where are you from?*
we have only shallow answers.
How must it feel to walk paths
familiar to great grandparents,
to grow into a place, your settlement?

Seasonal

The chill of September mist
fingers and wraps the garden,
hushing rustle and birdsong.
It closes off the sky—
the sun is blanketed away
pushing against it, willing it
to let go, to melt, to let
heat in again to finish
burnishing the fruit still
on the trees, softening
the skin of windfalls until
they subside into mush.
There will be time enough
for winter cold—let the mist's
grip loosen, sunshine slip through.

*

Up on the hill the blue tractor pulls
its red machinery across the field
to lift and pile rectangular packed bales.

Tracks left across the stubble are perfect lines—
equidistant and parallel—until the plough begins
to cut and turn the land into new patterns.

These rhythms anchor me, unchanged since childhood
when we ran scared stiff behind the combine—
a rattling beast spewing out streams of grain.

Hedges are heavy with brambles, red haws gleam,
jet beads of elderberries attract
a noisy rush of starlings—enough colour

to sustain us, to see us through the winter.
Though seasons merge and out-of-season rivers
burst their banks, harvest still insists
that this is autumn—our time for gathering in.

*

On my way home a far-off shout disturbs
the stillness of the dark back lane.
I quicken pace—another, closer,
but not ahead nor quite a shout—
the guttural cry is high above me
in the night sky. Fear shifts into joy.
I listen hard. I almost hear
the air pressed down, the muscular rhythm,
creak and beat of heavy wings.
The neck-stretched call comes again,
as welcome as the first swift in May.
I bless these sturdy flyers, navigating
darkness with their guiding honks.
Their arrival marks our Autumn, they leave
as we warm into Spring. Winter comforters,
reminding how the old patterns persist—
geese drawing their skeins across the sky,
people looking up to the unexpected call
for centuries, heartened and consoled.

*

Look up—high above the woods
the buzzards are displaying.
Wings still, they circle wide then
drop, twisting as they plummet,
then lift—see—back into the clouds.

Here, the gorse's yellow shouts
regeneration. That tiny dot
above you is a lark, surprising
you with showers of liquid song.

Now in the distance—listen,
the curlew's wavering notes
begin—a lament, its elusive
falling cadence finds you out,
phrasing like heart ache.

Safety Net

How will we keep our courage
as the body grows more frail
no longer a safe house—

fear is a new prison

How keep our hope
when they wage war
by withholding
aid, food, love
from the children—

I am looking for something
to hold me—

fifty-seven starlings lined up
on the wire
punctuate Autumn chattering
with whistles and squawks—

they will sweep up
into a net—
weave
a swirling hammock—
as they have always done
and for this brief moment

lift me with them

Lindisfarne Voices

Today the wind is sweeping all the sounds
we make back to the mainland.
It picks up distant voices, blows them close:

the holy chants of brothers brought by faith
from western shores, who crossed their sea
in currachs to reach this sacred place;

the foreign tongues of craftsmen from the east—
from Gaul and from the Rhinelands
they brought new skills in glass and metal;

and then the shouts, the creak of oars—
from the north the traders came,
hauling sturdy longboats through the waves.

They followed the flocks of Brent geese,
and sanderling—the island's rocky shore
their first landfall, the wide bay, a haven.

Low February sun is dazzling. In the blur
a flock of dunlin turns with the wind,
a curlew cries, godwits and plovers

pick over the shoreline, birds of passage,
transient visitors still wintering here.

A Frankish Craftsman's Letter from Lindisfarne

They sent me here in exile as if
cold Northern lands would make me forget.
They thought bleak pewter skies would freeze
away my love. They did not know that
summer has a different palette—now
every colour is reminding me of you.
There are banks of pink flowers just the shade
of your Sunday dress—the silk I brought you
from the East—and creamy foxgloves recall
the fine wool of your shawl. I saw
a butterfly as orange as your favourite
jelly, its dots like crumbs of sweet bread—
and you would have marvelled to see it
alight upon the richest purple flower.
Such colours! But it is blue that I must
tell you of, for blue is hope—the sea's
deep indigo, the sky's aquamarine,
and between the clouds—not pewter
but the white of your fair skin—
in the sweetest, palest blue I find
your eyes. Have faith, my love. Keep true.
In Autumn when the geese fly south
I will find a way to cross the sea to you.

After It Was Over

Did they understand the tides?
Did one man follow the moon's cycle
to plot their passage across the sea?

Did no-one see the longboats coming—
oars cutting the waves, fierce prows
driving through the cross currents?

Was there no warning in the soft curve
of the dunes, in the wind feathering
the grasses, rippling the seedheads?

Were the brothers all at prayer,
drawn close in contemplation,
in quiet work with vellum and fine brushes?

And after it was over, who was left
to see the stretching blue of sky—

and the larks, who was left to hear
the larks, silvering the air with their song?

Interiors

—after Edward Hopper

In the Café

She holds the handle tight as if she means to raise the cup, to drink.
Back to the window, she sits alone, facing the other clientele.
If they were looking they would note the fur trim on her coat,
the way the rich green fabric drapes, the fashionable hat.
If close enough they would appreciate her careful make-up—
lips ripe cherry, lashes soft and sooty, smooth pancake cheeks.

She does not look at them—her eyes are focused on the cup she doesn't lift.
They cannot see how she concentrates on sitting still, on steadying.
They cannot see the day is not holding, that days will never
hold their place, nor follow one another as they used to.

They cannot see her fingers whiten on the handle, how she pretends
to be a woman in a coat and hat with perfect make-up,
how she is holding tight against the pull of darkness
where someone howls, and time is gashed and broken.

From the Bridge

i.

The woman in the top floor window
doesn't know she is being watched.

It's early. The city is not awake.
Her night was restless—sticky—troubled.

She pulled on her cotton robe, hoped to leave
her worries in the unmade bed.

Craving cool air, she raised the sash,
sat on the sill, did not look down.

She is waiting for a breeze, some movement
in the heavy air. What is outside

does not concern her. She does not see
the footbridge, does not expect anyone

to be walking there—or standing now,
as if caught by the white of her gown.

ii.

And the nightwalker on the footbridge?
He paced away the hours, pushed through the dusk

until dawn, past shuttered shops, low-lit diners,
stopping only to light a cigarette,

to lean for a breath against a doorway,
fingers restless with the coins in his pocket.

The sleeping city draws him, lures him in,
with its shutters and blinds, curtains closed.

Each building hides its story, encloses
the lives that will begin again at sunrise.

He sees almost no one, keeps to the shadows—
never meets a glance, nor answers a greeting.

Pausing on the footbridge, the white caught his eye—
white like a veil—a sail—white like an angel's wing.

Building at Dusk

At dusk two lives appear in counterpoint
in the lit rectangles of sash windows.

A woman at a table turns her head
away from her book, surprised by a sound—

a voice—a summons. Her head turns to listen,
her body stays with the book's elsewhere.

She is not willing to leave the haven—
safe place conjured by the lines of words.

Next door, with blind half lowered, a young man
stares down, is held by the street below.

This moment before nightfall captures him.
He is eager for whatever it will bring.

He knows nothing of escape, nor refuge.
He knows only the here and now of waiting.

Automat

Behind her the window looks out on darkness.
How empty the street is—too late for
the hurry of workers heading home, for
crowds leaving cinemas and shows.

No one else there—no voice to distract from
the hums and whirrs, clicks and rumbles as chillers
switch on and off, thermostats regulate
to keep the food hot in the wall of glass boxes.

She sits with her back to the night, lit by
bright strip lights. She never looks up at
the absence of people at vacant tables,
the absence of anyone. She sits on,
spotlit in a drama with nobody watching.
How empty the street is in the hour before dawn.

July Visit

It's time again to harvest blackcurrants.
Their dangling clusters—awkward on thin stems,
at unexpected intervals along the branch—
demand a careful picking. I cannot do it
without remembering your last time here—
how you offered help but were longing
to escape into a book; how I would look up
to see you on the bench, freed for a while
from all your burdens, and you would lift
a vague hand in salute. I didn't know
it was your last visit—so much we could have said.
Picking now, I look up often, just in case.
It would be like you to pop back unannounced—
my fingers slip and squash the fruit, stain purple.

Poem for Jan

Away from home when you were leaving,

    I walked along lush Suffolk lanes

out of contact, all signals lost—

    I should have read the message

in the swathes of blue forget-me-nots.

For flowers blessed your passing, late spring

    the kindest time for you to go—

a blackbird's song, trees in new leaf,

    sending you gently.

Flowers chosen with love accompanied you—

    from hedgerows, cow parsley and sweet cicely,

bluebells and wild garlic from the woods;

from gardens the prettiest blush

    of apple blossom, honesty

for your own clear truth,

and always—

unfading—

the message of forget-me-nots.

Saying Goodbye to a Shakespeare Scholar

I thought that he had left already,
curled on his side, cheek pillowed on his palm.
So small now, all flesh gone, skin thinned—
translucent, uncreased, as if new.
All still until his eyes opened,
vague blue sharpening into focus.
There you are, he said. Then sleep returned.

The bed—so like a cot with metal sides,
thick rubber mattress—was too stark
for ninety-year old bones. He deserved
a softer nest—sheep's wool, perhaps,
collected from the hedgerows, thistledown,
a scattering of dried lavender and sage—
a Forest of Arden resting place to ease
the passing of a kind and wise old man.

Memorial

Nothing is moving in your flat—
just the silent sift of dust.

In the wardrobe your clothes take on
the droop of hangers, as if resigned.

The air—closed up for months—has
a fusty unwashed smell. No one

has been to brush dead flies from
windowsills, to clear away the parched

geranium. No one has plumped cushions,
straightened rugs—your shape is still

imprinted on that favourite chair,
where you sat to watch the world.

Where is the brisk cleaner bringing
mop and bucket, to open windows,

scrub and throw away? She would
fold up your clothes with care, smile

and remember the shared jokes—
your Saturday afternoon racing,

your delight in the oldest films.
She'd see your shoes and coats found

good homes, but would wonder what to do
with all those books. She'd sweep out

neglect and desolation, leaving the flat
agleam with *Pledge*, a little loved again.

Ward 15

The old people are resting in their bays—
beached in sheltered coves or calm inlets
where the sea may murmur and waves lap.
One alone far out calls and calls for help,
knows he is drowning. Another marooned
on a rock of silence refuses
to answer the husband trying to reach her,
to keep her afloat with his ring of words.

Visitors are unsettled, seeing their own futures
in the fearful elderly who are weak now
in body, some adrift in their minds.
Let there be eider ducks, bright puffins,
an occasional seal to break surface
in these hushed bays, these last safe harbours.

A&E

Midday heat is trapped between
low ceiling and a rubbery floor.
No windows. Swing doors flap open
for the constant traffic of trolleys
carrying the frail and frightened
wrapped in blankets, trailing tubes.
We are waiting for something to happen.

Our seats are sticky plastic. There is no air.
A girl with a black eye and bruised cheek
huddles as far away as possible
from a youth who snores and sprawls across
three chairs. A pregnant woman weeps.
A man holds up his hand in a salute,
blood seeping through the jaunty tea towel.

Wearing boxer shorts and tweed cap backwards,
a drunk is wheeled in. We sense diversion.
He lurches from his wheelchair, hops barefoot
towards the shop, grabs fistfuls of crisps,
then slips and falls, is stranded—a big red
bawling boy. Two neat nurses pull him up,
remove his swag. Raising her voice above

his roared obscenities, the Sister declares
he will not be treated if he can't behave,
in a tone of no-nonsense nanny.
We want to cheer and stamp our feet
as he subsides into scowling toddler,
groaning and petulant. The show is over.
We settle back to waiting to be seen.

In Praise of Makers and Dreamers

—for Ian Hird

Our country has become a waiting room
grey and airless and we cannot see outside.

Rain is closing in. We do not know
what we are missing, until we hear

a man begin to speak in a quiet voice.
A potter, he is moved to tell us,

to share with us, the secrets of his craft—
how he draws upon his region,

its creatures, plants, and history,
reviving ancient signs and patterns;

how he presses seed heads, oats and barley,
into the many-coloured local clay,

borrows shapes of prehistoric deer,
adds hare and curlew, swift and salmon—

his beloved land, the past and Nature
all living in his work. And as he speaks

the windows clear to show a view of hills,
then woods and fields of grain, old paths.

Mist lifts and the sky is beginning to be blue.
Soon we must get up and try the door.

November 14th 2015

In the steady rain a woman is planting,
bending to push smooth bulbs into the earth.

Ignoring the creep of cold she is planting
small promises into a day that is lacking light.

She is thinking of the spring morning when she will
discover her bulbs have released their straight stems,

their buds safe in furls of leaf; another, when warmth
will make the buds swell and open—petals

waxy scarlet, frilled pink, striped red and white—
then wider still to show the most intimate shapes

of anther, stamen, stigma—proclaimers of hope,
regeneration. These bulbs are her prayers,

nature's cycle her resistance to
the sunless days of suicide belts and bullets.

Pina Bausch

Her skin slips across her bones like silk
as if she has forsaken flesh and blood.

Her skeleton ripples, articulates; limbs
bend into angles of pain; grace becomes

near dislocation, smooth movement
turns staccato, control is breaking.

She is desolation, then passion, desire.
Her body is cutting emotion into air.

She could not speak this. There might be
a tune for it but words will not do.

Her skin slips across sternum, clavicle,
rib cage, sinews and tendons stretching

as if straining towards hope, but it is
anguish she dances, anguish and loss.

Paul Nash's Trees

Because he loved the trees he gave them
the finest detail that his brush
could render. He understood the way
a breeze makes branches dance, the play
of light on leaves, the shifting patterns
of the canopy against the sky.
He could catch the froth of spring time,
autumn's slow burn, revisiting
his favourite clumps like old friends.

And so, how else could he record
the horror of the Menin Road but as
an avenue of blasted trunks, of stumps
and splintered limbs—a landscape smashed.
The life force—the spark from root to bud—
was stamped out. He painted line after line
of mutilated trees, his brush repeating
frozen shapes, the petrified monuments
where once a breathing wood had been.

Ruins between Bernafay Wood and Maricourt: A Bedfordshire Corporal Reflects, July 1916

What struck us straightaway was how
the place looked so like home—
the wood just like the one where
we would camp, climb trees, set traps,
all the things that country lads will do.

And it was a miracle how well
the wood had stood up to these years
of war—some trees on the perimeter
were shattered stumps, but deep inside
all was green and growing strong.

Then the briqueterie, as they called it—
brickworks to us—its chimneys, cranes
and kiln just like the works at home.
We talked about it—us Bedfordshire lads—
rattled by it. It took us back, unsettled us.

So when the order came to destroy
it all, flatten the buildings, set
the whole wood ablaze with cordite shells,
we had to fight our feelings,
remember orders have to be obeyed.

Being a soldier means closing
your heart to the world you knew before,
not minding the charred and twisted trees,
the smashed-up rubble of people's lives,
the way war turns the land to barren waste.

Reclamation Instructions

Cellar

You will need to take the key down
from its hook, then push it far
into the lock. Jiggle it in place—
it won't turn easily. Open the door.
On the wall to your left is the switch—
white, ceramic—turn the central knob.
The light flickers on and the switch
starts ticking. The knob clicks back
second by second. You don't have long.
Be careful the door doesn't slam
behind you. The dark would be absolute,
would choke you with its musty velvet.

No handrail and each riser too deep.
The bulb is fizzing. Remember what
you have come for. The rippling snakes
are pipes lagged in frayed sacking.
You walk into cobwebs furred thick
with dust—they catch in your hair,
stick to your fingers. Tea chests teeter
against the wall. Dare you feel inside?
Something rustles against your ear.
Perhaps it isn't here—time ticks away.
You will not linger if the light goes
out. You are breathing too much loss.

Ground Floor

You won't find much remaining
on this floor—though, the sooty smudges
in the alcove may suggest a stove.
(Do you see a coke-fired Rayburn,
acrid fumes escaping
each time the fire is fed, and
a patchwork of sleepy cats pressed
to its heat?) The scullery door sticks—
quarry tiles lifting as the roots
of poplar trees push their way in,
undermining—foundations shifting,
walls out of kilter, cracks spreading.

What could be left in the larder?
Stores of hazel nuts hollowed out
by field mice, a rusty meat safe.
Whatever you came for isn't here.
Don't push the lounge door—someone
nailed it shut from the other side,
set up camp there until wind and rain
shoved the French windows in, mouldered
the carpet to sodden sponge, ballooned
the paper off the walls—(chosen,
perhaps, from a book of samples
to set off salmon pink curtains.)

First Floor

Be careful at the turn of the stairs—
the bannister is missing.
You know which room to leave till
last—but first go into the pink room.
Under the dust shroud can you smell
(just faintly) the scents of seventeen—
cheap hair lacquer, Miners make-up,
freesia perfume—and if you listen
hard you'll catch the muffled whispers,
Saturday night confidences,
a safety net of words till dawn
in the rickety double bed.

Beyond here the passage is not safe.
Go back to the room you fear
to enter, the curtains still closed.
See, shapes are familiar—
wardrobe, tallboy, dressing table.
Did you get a whiff of powder—
faded rose or crushed violet?
Do not think of neglect. What you
are tasting is desolation.
The air in here is thick with it.
It lies heavy on your chest,
the weight of such solitary pain.

Attic

Carry it with you to the attic.
Up here everything is broken.
Watch your footing—a crow softens
into dust and feathers where it fell.
Books lie splayed, spines split open.
A cot in the corner is full of rubble,
nursery lambs and rabbits still
skipping their way along the bars.
The glass in those family photos
is cracked, the paper foxed. Lift them
to the light. Look into their eyes—
young men forgotten, left behind.

No air—raise your arm, hit out,
punch the ceiling hard, see how
the plaster falls in a white storm,
bare laths splinter. Make a bigger hole
and the crow will gather his feathers,
escape. Shut your eyes tight and you
can let those young men go too—out
through the roof to a better past.
And the one who brought her pain in
through the door alone? Time to set
her free—think of a Chagall painting—
send her with flowers, out into the blue.

Wednesday Afternoons

He stands at the counter watching for her bus.
She is nearly six. She knows the stop.
A cigarette burns away in his mouth.
He has his coat on in the office cold.
They will go to a café for lunch.
She will skip beside him. He will not hold her hand.
The usual waitress will make a fuss of her.

Once back he will lift the hinged counter
to let her through. He will not lift her over.
He will light the gas fire then,
settle her in the large office chair with paper
and the heavy stamps and ink pads that she loves.
Her chatter will bounce off his silence.

When the men come in from finished jobs
they will tease until she is flushed and almost tearful,
ask her questions about school, take her
on a tour of the fusty furniture, if she wants to go.
They bring her milky sweet tea in a dirty mug.
They seem to like the babble of her words.

All this he witnesses from his usual place
in his coat, standing at the counter under
the weight of unpaid bills, the columns of figures
that never add up, the piles of yellowed pages never filed,
unanswered enquiries, accounts never settled; under
the blight of damp spreading through the warehouse,
furring sofas and mattresses with mould.

At five-thirty they will put on coats and hats.
She will get the buttons wrong, the hat askew.
They will lock the office door, check the shutter.
On the bus her short legs will struggle up the stairs.
He will light a cigarette, open his newspaper—
her chatter nearly lost in the engine's roar.

Halfway Houses County Primary

Just when the security of shorts and T-shirts,
scuffed sandals and tree-climbing became less sure—
her body uncertain in its new softness,
folded arms a shield for her tender chest—
she was moved to a different school.

No uniform to blend her in, she watched herself
in the noisy playground, stiff legs, closed throat,
swallowing words back. Behind her the small safe school
where no one shouted, hit or spat, where mild
elderly teachers eased them into reading, writing, sums.

It was a lost world. She could never go back. Here was
the world of Edward Beckham, his too-big boots and no socks
to his name, who couldn't read but had furious fists,
a good left foot.
          And Irene Cottington,
the eldest of ten, her thin skin tight over pointy bones,
wild brown curls, a faded cotton dress and wellington boots on
the coldest day, her legs chapped red, but so nimble and light
at skipping, at netball, at shinty.

She could do the lessons—she picked up the new routines—
but really she knew nothing at all. She kept her head down,
watched and listened, held back, waiting to be accepted.
She learnt a new language but could never find the words
to tell them about school when she got home.

Before

Remember how it felt when the long days stretched
into evening and no one called you home,
and you wandered down the hill as cool air
breathed up from the grass and a star shone in blue sky—

when you opened the back door so tired
that every pore of your skin seemed to buzz
with nettle stings, gnat bites, scrapes and rashes,
and your mother took one look and called you
a ragamuffin, and you couldn't even get
the words out to say yes, you would like
a jam sandwich and a glass of milk—

and though it wasn't bath night till Sunday
she ran a warm bath for you because
you couldn't get into bed with those filthy feet,
but you squealed and moaned when she rubbed
the soapy flannel over your legs and arms
prickling with sunburn and scratches and scabs,
and she laughed as she pulled burrs and sticky jack
out of your hair and rolled you in a rough towel—

remember how it felt to put on clean pyjamas,
to get into bed smelling of Knights Castile,
to fall into a deep dark pit of sleep
while she was still talking—

The Girl That She Was

Her Bedtime

She waited for the owl's ghostly call
to float across from the dark copse,
ancient and sad, it soothed her,
its tune unchanging, like the stars
she knew were still there underneath
the clouds. The girl that she was
leaned far out into the night
to find those three bright stars,
the studs in Orion's belt.
She lay awake listening for rain,
soft rain that stirred the leaves
of the spreading blossom tree outside
her window. Too old at nine for lullabies,
she longed to slip into sleep to that sound.

Nightriding at Twelve

Her front beam lights a narrow pathway through
the dark. She pedals hard to keep it bright,
the dynamo's whirr like a humming insect
on her tail, almost a comfort, though
it threatens to shut out the other sounds
she needs—waves lapping on shingle,
the eerie clinking of catamarans—
sounds to navigate by as she stares ahead,
alert for movement, knees burning. No houses
for a mile or two—she wishes she could still

pretend she was a princess galloping
over hill and dale on her Arab steed.
Instead, she can only grip the handlebars
with sweaty fingers all the way home.

Land Lock

The girl that she was walked the cliff path
on blustery Sundays, when the sea
churned and foamed—no blues or greens,
just seething brown like café au lait,
the mud all stirred up, as she was.
She let the wind tie knots in her hair,
force tears down her face, and her cries
were swallowed in the waves' crash.
She shouted at the world and the wind
took her words—but now where can she take
the rage, the same pain that is closing
her throat, hurting her chest—where are
the cliff tops now, the angry waves?

The Tricks Dreams Play

I thought I had woken suddenly
in that teenage-girl-bedroom you made
for me in the house we neither of us liked—

where the ponytailed girls on the wallpaper
said I had to cross over, I had to be
grown up now—
                I thought I had woken and
I was afraid. I knew I must sift through the fear.

If it was the house—
                    the empty rooms,
the absence of the voices that were loudest,
the absence of the ones most likely to speak out,
argue, take hold—

                if it was the silence, the sense
that all was not well but you wouldn't say—
then I would just have to lie there or try
to sleep and hope that the whispering voices
did not hiss in my ears.

                  But if it was the other
sort of danger—the man with a file or
some tool to jemmy open the window,
then climb in and creep through the rooms
for something that he wouldn't find—
I could go and wake you.

                  But the dream melted then
leaving only the backwash of dazed loneliness
we lived in, you and I, in the draughty house.

Night Visitor

At once she is awake. She can't tell
if the thuds she hears are in her chest or
there's another burglar at the back door.

On her feet and listening—in the pretty
baby dolls her mother brought her
that last weekend visit, she is freezing.

The sounds are outside. She feels her way
along the passage to her father's room,
his snores a regular rattling tune.

She pauses, not used to going in—
the parents' bedroom always forbidden.
Has she ever woken him? The door creaks.

Dad? Dad! The snores erupt, subside.
He sits up blinking in the sudden light.
There's someone trying to get in again.

She feels like crying, but this is not the time.
He's up and pulling on a sweater, slippers.
Stay here. I'll go and see. She listens hard.

Doors are opening, back door unlocking.
Her mother's things are on the dressing table—
the box of powder, the fluffy pink puff,

the line of Revlon nail varnishes—all red.
If she opened the wardrobe her best dresses
would be there too, waiting. She shivers.

He's coming back. She hears him chuckle.
Come and see. Here. He wraps a cardigan
around her. It smells of *Coty L'Aimant.*

They stand in the doorway, close
but not touching. A big dark shape
is lumbering through the flowerbed.

It lifts its head, then goes on grazing.
*One of Johnson's donkeys—you can ride it
home if you like.* Relief is bubbling up.

He lights a Players, locks the door.
Back to bed now, Scamp. On her way through
the cold house she pushes her arms into
the cardigan sleeves, pulls it round her, tight.

Cat Security

Billy is still looking for the honey badgers.
They escaped last night in the corner of the lounge.

While they were making their attempt at breaking out
he stood on hind legs, stretched his body tall to block
the screen, batting and swiping to keep the creatures in.

But he knows they got out, and scans the bookshelves
for a trace of beady eye, retractable claw.

He's raced up and down the stairs enough times
to be sure they can't be lurking in the bedroom,
so he settles beside me with an accusing stare,

as if wondering why I ever let them in,
and what fierce interloper he'll have to deal with next.

Poem

My mother is distrustful of dreams,
will only make rare cameo appearances—

just turning a corner, leaving a room,
out of sight as I run after her.

Instead, like a guerrilla gardener, she slips
into that other place, where poems start.

She scatters a few seeds, digs a hole
and buries something—a root, a tuber,

a shaggy rhizome—then fades. I do not
see her go. The surface seems untroubled

and I am already less sure of the spot.
I must not dig down to find it, must wait,

for it is only when I have no memory
of her action that her gift will grow.

Two Mothers

She is tiny, shrunken as if
the metal bed has sucked her in,
hidden her body in its rubber mattress.

Her cheeks have hollowed. Someone
has combed her hair the wrong way.
Her fists are clenched.

I wipe the trickle of saliva
from her chin and know she would
hate to be seen like this.

She should be in scarlet, or
kingfisher blue, hair set, nails done,
a touch of lipstick—and talking,

laughing, martini glass in hand.
I cannot tell her I am pregnant, but
I must keep thinking of the baby

and the toddler left at home
to anchor me, for I am out of my depths—
without them I am in danger

of becoming a small child again,
hanging on to her mother's coat,

not letting go.

Fledge

Blown from its nest
the collared dove was stranded—
legs damaged, tail as yet unfeathered.
The parents hovered, perching above,
settling beside, unable to reverse
the catastrophe, calling.

Three days of vigilance—
I tiptoed past, watching
its ungainly crawl for cover,
perfect wings spreading, useless.
In sleep, it was a soft buff pillow
half-hidden under ferns.

The fourth day, just a puff of cream down—
perhaps at first light, urged on,
the strong wings beat enough to lift
it high—perhaps they circled,
the three together, climbing,
with their eerie, wavering cry.

How I need to believe in its flight—
small dove freighted with so much hope.

Porthcurno 1982

Will it be like that time the sea
pulled me away from the shallows,

(the water a seductive turquoise
over crushed white shell-sand, lapping,
lapping, as if a safe place)

caught me in its current and my arms
and legs fought against it, every muscle
refusing, and I clawed my way back

to the edge where my two little boys
waited, holding my beach towel ready?

Mirror

These mornings you can't be sure whose face
you'll find looking back from the mirror.
There are so many women jostling.

Some days the whirling mum returns,
juggling P.E. kits and dinner money,
a toppling pile of essays to be marked.

Some days you're forty-seven and moving
on, new love filling the empty rooms, building
shelves for books that overflow their boxes.

Then there are nights when your mother appears,
taking you by surprise with her solidity,
you, young and wispy, not quite in focus.

You wake, you are twenty-seven,
the weight of a baby's head still warm
against your arm—into a stretching space

where you must catch the ends of threads,
twist them into a rope to pull you back
to now, today, your seventy-year-old face.

Three Score Years and Ten

and she is like one of those winter apples
late on the tree,
skin already puckered
as the flesh grew soft,
then softer.

She is surprised
that wrinkled skin isn't tough.
It is thin,
thinning fast, splits easily,
hurts.

No elasticity,
no resistance,
so brittle it cannot
protect the core—
her heart—

how it rattles,
battered by all the storms
of the troubled world.

Night Watching

A child, she would kneel at the window
staring into the dark, waiting for fox
or weasel, sudden scurry of shrew or vole,
drawn to the garden's unfamiliar contours,
the way they excluded her. And now again,
this two a.m. garden is not hers.
It belongs to the owls, netting it with shrieks,
to whatever rustles under the hedge
shuffling the leaves, rolling the apples—
so carefully raked and tidied—back on the grass.
Always her lodestar, this desire
to touch the edges of the wild world,
observing its creatures—and one day staying
still enough to dissolve there, like mist.

Now

Now it matters more that there are stars,
that deserts hide the fossils of sea creatures,
that ridge and furrow traces mark the fields,
and from deep below the city streets
diggers turn up skeletons and tools.

Closer now to ending than beginning,
stars provide a particular kind of comfort
for black-edged days of hospitals
and funerals. The night sky asserts
You are temporary—a pond skater
skidding across surfaces. And it doesn't
matter when there are these constellations,
and the soothing continuity of the moon.

Gone

If she is not there in the morning,
you will find her at the field's edge
watching for the tumbling flight of lapwings.

On summer evenings she lights the lamp,
waits for the soft wings of moths
to brush their dust against her window.

Do not look for her in the night.
She will be at the wood's border
listening out for the tawny owls' call.

She wants to make her bed in dry leaves,
lie down with the scuffle of hedgehogs,
the tiny tracks of the hazel dormouse.

Conservation

She keeps the roof tight, the walls secure,
maintains the fabric as best she can,

alert to slippage, cracks and damp—
a duty handed on by the old man

who left her rusty clinker and smashed pots
to surface as reminders from the earth.

The garden is trying to go back to grass.
She bargains—allows hawkbit, coltsfoot, daisies

to stay among the scabious and flocks.
But every shower revives the buttercups, the mares' tails.

They are pushing back against her interlopers.
They would return her ordering to wildness—

to wilderness—in weeks. She must learn to tread
more lightly, to let go. She is only
a temporary caretaker passing through.

Naming the Beasts

Fifteenth Century

An icon shows the beasts all crowding up
as if eager for names to settle them in place.
Adam points to each—birds eating berries
become magpie, crow, peacock; the orange beast
with lustrous mane is lion; grinning monkey
rides an elephant; horse and deer run ahead
of panting camel, and in the foreground,
fully stretched, is snake. In his exuberance
the artist adds a dragon waiting to be named.

Nineteenth Century

High in the canopy, a first explorer
catches a flash of scarlet at the periphery
of his vision, shape and colour unrecorded,
till then unseen; a monkey, almost familiar,
but longer limbed, too new to have a kind,
a category written down. On the forest floor
are grubs and insects innumerable,
an entire beetle species to be given
a name by this latter-day Adam.

Twenty-first Century

What could we tell artist and explorer
about our time? How explain our lack of care,
our inattention, our failure to protect?
Their worlds were overflowing with abundant life.
We draw up lists of endangered and extinct.
Habitats are shrinking, the forests burning.
Loss is the legacy we're leaving;
the names disappearing from our language.

My Arctic

—after reading Barry Lopez

My mind is travelling across the Arctic
before it is too late. My tongue is testing
tundra permafrost glacier orca narwhal.
I am led through a locked winter, see how muskoxen
scraping snow from moss and willow buds sustain hare
and ptarmigan—
                on into a spring surprising
with the constant passage of migrating creatures,
with lichen answering light and thaw, insects rising
in buzzing clouds and snow buntings lining their nests
with muskox fur. How the pieces interlock!

                I am not thinking about
hunters whalers trappers rifles knives harpoons.
My mind is travelling across a place where the only sounds
are the calls of birds and animals—no intrusions—
where the glaciers are not melting, where blue
is a multitude of blues to tread softly in,
                      to rest in, be lost in

Synapse Failed

First a falter,

    then the rhythm stumbles.

A gap is opening

      between *then* and *now*—

    they slide out of reach.

It is not like forgetting

      which month or day,

when a rope of remembering

      pulls you back—

more like a fissure

      to fall down—

you are suspended nowhere—

      and who are you?

Then a jolt sets it off again

      you claw your way back—

slowly *now* follows *then*

      again, the gaping hole fades.

What if there were no jolt

        to reset time's ticking?

Terminus

I am waiting for the bus to leave
houses behind—for the road to become
an intrusion, enclosed on each side
by hedges splashed cream with blossom,
bordering fields where pasture has
turned into scrub and tussocks for
a herd of rough horses, manes tangled
with brambles and thistledown.

I am waiting for the driver to shout
Terminus—for the road to become
a lane narrowing ahead to
a single file track where I must walk
by myself into the waiting wood.

Here, with the dainty footfall of
fallow deer, the startled clack
of the gaudy cock pheasant, darkness
will bring the flicker of moth flight,
and always the tawny owl's call.
This is the destination, among
tree roots and lichen, where
nothing is asked for,
                       everything given.

Acknowledgements

Thanks are due to the editors of the following publications where some of the poems first appeared:

ARTEMISpoetry, Magma, The North.

'Before' was published on the *Diamond Twig* website.

'Ruins between Bernafay Wood and Maricourt' was included in *Poems for Screaming Steel: Art, War and Trauma*, Newcastle Centre for the Literary Arts/The Hatton Gallery, 2014.

'Lindisfarne Voices' was first published in a pamphlet, *Waves and Bones,* Newcastle Centre for the Literary Arts, 2018.

'Terminus' was first published in a pamphlet, *Lovely, Dark and Deep,* Grey Hen Press, 2021.

With thanks to Sheila Wakefield, Founder and Editor at Red Squirrel Press, and to Linda France, Jackie Litherland, and the Newcastle Women's Poetry Group.

A NOTE ON THE TYPES

This book is set primarily in Mercury Text, a contemporary
serif from the Hoefler&Co digital type foundry in New York,
which describes the type as a 'bright and sparkling' typeface
'originally designed for the hardscrabble world of newspaper
printing.' Versatile and readable, it makes a fine choice in its
functional clarity for setting poetry.

Titles and epigraphs are set in Metro Nova, Toshi Omagari's
contemporary updating of W. A. Dwiggins' Metro Number 1.